INHABIT
YOUR
Joy

A BOOK OF NUDGES

ELENA A. SONNINO

Elena Sonnino,
illustrations by Kaira Boston

Elena Sonnino Life Coaching
www.elenasonnino.com

Inhabit Your Joy: A Book of Nudges by Elena A. Sonnino—1st ed.

Paperback: 979-8-9853267-0-3
Hardcover: 979-8-9853267-1-0

DEDICATION

To the doctor that invited me to inhabit my joy.

And to life's treasures.

INTRODUCTION

I remember my dad once saying to me that I was always someone who could do anything I set my mind to.

I love my dad. But over the years I've realized that he was only partially correct. Because my mind was never the key.

The key was something even more powerful.

The key was how I inhabited my dreams. How I inhabited my truest self.

How I inhabited my joy.

Inhabiting my joy came easily for me.

Except when it didn't.

On those days — which, let's be clear, were entire seasons of my life — I was my own worst enemy. Because as natural as it might be for me to inhabit my joy, I'm also an Olympic-level catastrophizer and overthinker.

Which is why I can tell you without a shadow of a doubt (and as the daughter of a neurosurgeon) that inhabiting your joy has NOTHING to do with your brain. (Sorry, Papi.)

Yes, your brain is powerful. And yet this book has very little to do with the brain.

The intention of this book, and my invitation to you, is to help you realign and reorient yourself to this key. Because it already lives inside you. It always has and always will.

The key to inhabit your joy...is YOU.

This key showed itself to me several years ago.

I've just started my day at school and I get a message to call my doctor's office.

I get on the phone, and he says, "I don't know how to tell you this, but you're pregnant."

My response might surprise you. Because at that moment, I'm angry and I start crying.

This should be the most exciting moment of my life. My entire life I'd dreamed of two things: to be a teacher and to be a mom.

But this was petrifying news because I've also been told that this was never something that would be possible. For years, I'd heard that I'd probably never get pregnant. And if I ever did it would not be a viable pregnancy.

My doctor heard my sobs and knew that these weren't happy tears.

And after a moment he said something I've never forgotten:

"You have a choice to make. You could grieve, or you could choose to celebrate until the day you can't."

As soon as he said it, I knew that I was going to celebrate. That I was going to choose to be on this journey no matter what. Without any real certainty.

This phone call is a big deal because, six years earlier, I handled another phone call very differently.

There I was, six years before. I'm in my bedroom inside my apartment.

The phone rings. This time it's my oncologist.

I have no idea the words he actually says, but the message is clear.

My Hodgkin's disease is back.

I'd been down this road before. The first time I'd stayed optimistic. Always hopeful. But at that moment, I was angry.

The room went black and I felt myself falling into this deep dark hole.

I entered what felt like my own personal war room and then proceeded to spend the next six months doing everything I possibly could to protect myself and survive cancer.

And I did. I survived.

But something else happened along the way.

I spent those next six years really, until that other phone call, in what I now call survival mode.

Looking over my shoulder. Wanting to move forward but always wondering.

Wondering if a cold was a symptom of a recurrence.

Wondering when it was going to come back.

Wondering when the other shoe was going to drop.

But that all changed when I made that choice to celebrate on that call.

As easy as that choice felt, I honestly had no idea where and how to begin to celebrate. So I took it one step at a time.

That first afternoon, celebrating looked like going to a nearby pharmacy to buy two things: a pregnancy test (because I wanted to see the double lines with my own eyes) and a journal — where I began to write letters to "my sweet baby" that very first day.

I didn't realize it at the time, but I was writing a new chapter in my life rooted in thriving instead of surviving.

Let me be honest: It took a good 10 years before I really started to be able to see the power of this choice for myself.

But when I did, I knew that I wanted to devote my life to helping other women learn to thrive.

You don't have to have gone through a cancer journey.

Because real talk: Many of us have traversed challenging moments. Difficult moments.

The first step is to decide that you don't want to be stuck in survival mode anymore. To decide that you want to thrive and start to explore what that feels and looks like for YOU.

Because here is a secret — it looks and feels different for each of us. And this isn't something we learn how to do in school.

But it is possible.

That is where Inhabit Your JOY comes in. It is THE KEY.

I want you to be able to live your life, fully alive.

To remember that YOU are the one you've been waiting for. To remember that your very best teacher already lives inside you.

My hope is that these nudges lift you up and help you create your own path to thriving, not just when life feels easy-peasy and fabulous but even on the hard and uncertain days.

WHY NUDGES? WHAT EVEN IS A NUDGE?

Real talk: My inclination is to go DEEP. In just about everything. I'm one of those people that can make meaning out of anything. This is a fabulous ability to have when you are a life coach but sometimes makes life more complicated than it needs to be.

Have I mentioned that I'm an Olympic-level overthinker and catastrophizer?

Send me a text that says "Please call me" and I'll likely start to wonder if I did something wrong.

Yes, I'm that person.

I'm also the person who starts worrying when I see a missed call from my dad in the middle of the night. (Which isn't really the middle of the night because he's in Italy and six hours ahead. And the call? It was a butt dial.)

Sometimes we just need a nudge. A gentle knock-knock to the heart. A reminder.

A nudge is concise. It meets you where you are. It is easily accessible. It turns your WALLS into windows or doorways.

A nudge is a pattern disruptor. It helps you take a step forward.

These nudges are organized into categories. Be rooted. Be curious. Be alive. Some of them apply to more than one category.

They are intended to help you get out of your head and access a moment of thriving and, yes, joy. Because the key to inhabiting your joy is to allow the big and the little moments of aliveness to touch your heart.

These nudges won't make the hard stuff go away. But they create an important disruption in all the mind activity (aka drama), which is sometimes all it takes to come back to what matters most.

And they might just help you savor the deliciousness of your life, one small moment at a time. And that, sweet friend, is how we THRIVE.

So yes, my inclination is to go deep. It is who I am. And yet, I have seen the power of these nudges as individual practices that you can access in the day-to-day of regular life to invite shifts and steps forward. Each of these nudges can be a practice in its own right. You may find one that you want to stay with as a practice over time or you can try one each day.

There is no wrong way to be "nudged."

Let me repeat that again, just in case you need it (consider this your first nudge): There is NO wrong way to be nudged or use this book or The Nudges inside it. Consider this your "I-cannot-get-this-wrong" permission slip.

I guess the only question now is, are you ready?

GET ROOTED

Grounded. Centered. Rooted.

What does that even mean?

Let's think for a moment.

What does it mean to be rooted?

If you are a tree or a plant, it means that you are attached and tethered to the earth by roots that draw up nutrients from the soil and help you grow.

If you are a person, rooted in a community — you probably feel connected to a group and feel like you belong.

If you are rooted in a belief, you believe that thing to your core.

If you are standing on one leg, being rooted or grounded means that you feel strong and balanced and able to maintain your stance.

I once had a client who described the result of her coaching journey with me as feeling like a redwood tree. She could be jostled but unmoved from her truths.

Another client described the journey as if she had become her own island. That it was okay for there to be storms because, as her own island, she has everything she needs.

The issue for most of us is that while we understand the value of being rooted in family and community, we forget that rootedness starts within us first.

And then...too often, we grow roots that aren't ours to grow. We take on beliefs, ideas, values, or ways of being that are passed down to us by others — or shoulds...or expectations.

So let's redefine what it means to be rooted and explore why it matters.

Being rooted creates a strong foundation. It is your starting point. Your core. It is home.

Being rooted creates a system of nourishment and nurturing.

If you think about it, every jump starts and ends somewhere. Every flight has a beginning and an end.

Simply put: Every time you inhabit your joy, it is as if you are opening your wings and flying.

And flying begins on the ground. The more rooted you are, the higher you can fly.

Let's get rooted.

THE NUDGE

Grab a pen and paper. Set a timer for 5 minutes.

Allow your thoughts, your feelings, your judgments — anything and everything that is taking up space in your brain — to be lovingly dumped onto the page.

The only rules are that this has to be written and there is no censoring yourself as you go.

Maybe you write a list or words or allow your stream of consciousness to flow out on the page.

You cannot get this wrong.

BE ROOTED #1
Get rooted in the present with a brain dump.

A brain dump is one of my GO-TO practices to come back to what matters. To create my starting point for any given day or moment.

Real talk: The beauty of a brain dump is that it helps you be rooted, be CURIOUS, and be alive in your life, just by showing up to the blank page. It makes sense that this all-purpose nudge be our headliner.

A brain dump is a gift you give yourself to notice how you are feeling. What you are thinking. What is on your mind?

It invites you to honor it all without judgment censoring. And then to lovingly give it a place to live (other than in your head), even if for just a moment.

A brain dump isn't about WHAT you write. I like to think of it as a decluttering practice that creates space for what matters and gives everything else a place to live that isn't in my brain.

THE NUDGE

Lie down for a moment anywhere that is easily available.
On your bed, on a yoga mat, on the grass.
(Can't lie down? You can do this standing up or seated in a chair.)

Allow yourself to be still, right where you are.
If it feels good you can take a breath.

Notice the support of the earth below you.
Allow your body (or legs) to feel heavy.

And then place your right hand on your belly
and your left hand on your heart.

Breathe. Notice. Feel your heartbeat.
Notice sensations as they make themselves known to you.
Feel the truth of you at this moment.

Whisper a "thank you" to yourself as you inhale
and receive it in your belly.

And then whisper "I love you" to yourself as you release
the exhale up to your heart.

BE ROOTED #2

Connect with your body.

I have a secret for you. Ok, it isn't a secret. But it is a fact that we love to forget.

Your body is wise.

Your body has wisdom for you to connect to. Your body knows things long before your mind does.

Most of us spend a lot of time talking TO our bodies. And more often than not, those monologues are not kind or loving. But when was the last time that you listened to your body? Felt its power? Its wisdom?

I love reminding clients that the sensations that our body has for us are benevolent messengers. That backache, gurgling in your stomach, or feeling in your hip is just your body trying to get your attention.

The problem is that we move so fast throughout the day that we judge instead of listen.

What if you decided to connect with your body? To see it as your ally? To love it as a container for your rootedness? As a home for your belongings?

THE NUDGE

Grab a journal and ask yourself,
What do I know for sure in this moment?

Make a list. Write it all down. Start with the facts.
Notice what comes up (and what doesn't). Notice how you feel.

Repeat this process any time you get caught up in
overthinking or are spinning in uncertainty around a decision.
Use it as a way to proactively be present, mindful, and intentional.

You can add "in this moment" to almost anything
to bring yourself back to the present. For example,
How does my body feel in this moment?
What am I craving in this moment?
What matters most in this moment?

BE ROOTED #3

What do you know in this moment?

Overthinking is a pattern that gets in our way and creates a spin-cycle that takes us away from our truth. This nudge is for you if you ever get caught up in what-ifs and uncertainty.

Getting rooted is about being present. In the moment. Noticing what is here for you NOW, instead of thinking about what happened yesterday or what might happen tomorrow.

Being rooted in the moment allows you to notice the three butterflies that are flying outside your window or the way your heart speeds up when you are doing something you love. It is an invitation to feel the feels and discern what is true in the moment and where your brain is turning a moment into an epic novel of what-ifs.

Here is how Holly feels about this nudge:

"When Elena offered me this nudge, it became one of the most powerful tools in my toolbox. It encourages me to get out of the swirling, negative thought cycles so that I can assess what is truly causing me anxiety as well as see the many blessings in my life, like when I had to navigate my daughter having a concussion. I was allowing the worst-case scenarios in my head to take control and fear was dictating my life. I journaled with this question and it brought clarity. Yes, we needed to focus on her healing, AND we had a great team of medical professionals and educators support-ing her. She would be okay, and I could move from thoughts of fear to those of trust. Every time I use this nudge it grounds me and allows me to feel more balanced."

THE NUDGE

Grab a piece of paper or journal and write the words

"I am...

I am...

I am...

I am...

I am...

I am..."

Fill in your I am statements with whatever feels TRUE

for you today. In this moment.

Maybe smile or offer yourself gratitude for each of your

I am statements.

BE ROOTED #4

I am...

You wear so many hats. You are ALL the things to ALL the people.

And none of those hats are the true YOU.

Real talk: The TRUE you is more than one thing. The experience of being alive and inhabiting your joy happens when you invite yourself to belong as a whole. All of you.

I love it when my clients or colleagues say things like, "Elena, you are so zen. You are so calm." Because every time I hear that, I think of my daughter or my husband who probably have a very different opinion of my energy — they'd likely describe me as impatient and prone to raising my voice. (Yes. It happens. I am both of those energies.)

I am Italian and Jewish. I also talk with my hands. I am also a mom, an intuitive, a gardener, a listener, and a yogini. All of those versions of me are true. And none of them define me.

I love to say that "becoming is mysterious." With each new day, what or WHO you are looks different. The more you get to know and connect with all of your parts, the more rooted you are. And the more rooted you are, the more you allow your TRUTH to nourish you.

Your TRUTH lives deep inside you. It is a state of being more than a "thing." And getting rooted in the full spectrum of your experience is a gift of belonging that you can give yourself.

THE NUDGE

Sink into child's pose. Breathe here.
Allow the earth to come up and meet you.

Feel the invitation of gravity to release anything you are holding on to
(that isn't yours). Invite yourself to BELONG, just as you are.

You might even repeat the mantra: "I am exactly where
I need to be in this moment" to yourself while you breathe.

Find a guide to the yin yoga shapes on page 95

BE ROOTED #5

Take a child's pose.

So often we seek out answers and clarity outside of ourselves.

We look for answers. For truths. For knowledge. For validation.

But the truth is that you are your own best teacher. And your body has everything it needs and craves.

Let me say that again in a different way: You are the thing you've been waiting for.

A child's pose is good for the days that I feel particularly spinny, indecisive, or out of alignment with my core values. But it is also delicious to honor and allow a moment to fill me. To just BE still and to find my inner sense of home.

The thing about a child's pose — where you sit on your heels and fold forward toward the earth — is that it helps you move from thinking into feeling. Feeling sensations. Feeling the rise and fall of your breath. Feeling the support of the earth below you. This shape cultivates a sense of stillness that invites you to dim the lights on ALL the noise so that you can come back to YOU.

THE NUDGE

Set a one-word intention for the day.

The reason to select one word to encapsulate your intention
is that it gives you something to prioritize.
Think of it as a one-word pledge that anchors you
and frames your journey so that you are less reliant
on outcomes or specific results.

You can start by asking yourself the question:
How do I want to feel when I
_____?
(Go to sleep tonight. Finish my meeting.
After my date. At the end of my workout.)

Write it down and come back to check in on it
throughout the day. And then at the end of the day,
notice where and how did you connect with that feeling?
With that intention?

BE ROOTED #6
Choose ONE word.

I realized something over my years as a coach and human: A whole LOT of us walk around perpetually unsatisfied with our lives. (And as our own worst enemies.)

If you are anything like me, or most of the women I work with, reaching a goal feels fabulous. But is usually followed by an immediate "what's-next" desire or — even worse — feeling perpetually unfulfilled.

Look, I ran a second marathon to prove that my first wasn't a fluke. And a third because I thought I was fitter and could beat my finish time. (We won't talk about what I was prioritizing during the fourth or fifth. Suffice it to say, my past running life wasn't very rooted or joyful.)

I'd love to offer the idea that your roots aren't nurtured by your goals. They aren't nourished by finish lines. Your roots expand and grow stronger when you tend to your WHY. To what matters. To what is important...to YOU.

Something shifts when you prioritize your WHY. When you prioritize how you want to feel as an intention. Intentions come from a place within you, rather than the expectations of friends, colleagues, or family.

Intentions ask you to consider how you want to feel. Maybe an income goal is about feeling freedom. Maybe a weight-loss goal is about strength or love. Maybe your goal to generate new leads is rooted in service or connection. When you find clarity about the way you want to feel at the end of the day, week, quarter, or year — you have a target that allows you to widen your scope and foster that intention in ways that might surprise you.

THE NUDGE

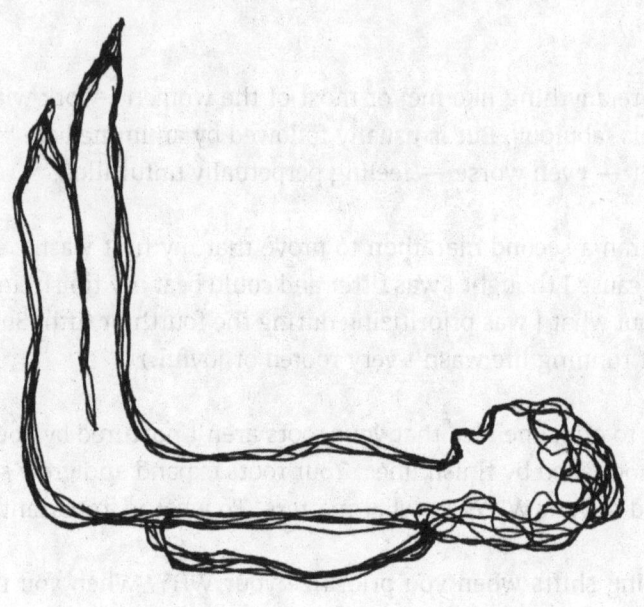

Find a guide to the yin yoga shapes on page 95

BE ROOTED #7

Take legs up the wall.

There we were. Five adult women. Five smart, adult women. And yet, in that moment, every single one of us in our own way was more nervous than we'd been in a very long time.

It was the day of our yoga teacher training final exam.

Despite a solid four months of preparation and a whole lot of practice and studying, my brain felt like a complete jumble of all the things. I was sure I was going to fail. The only thing that made me feel better was that, when I looked around at my friends, we all had that same dazed and confused look.

I don't remember whose idea it was. And I'm pretty sure that what happened next happened without words. As if gravity was calling us to the hallway, one by one, one pair of legs went up the wall and then another and another.

I can only speak for myself...but in that moment I didn't need words of encouragement. I didn't need my inner cheerleader to tell me all would be ok.

What I needed was to allow gravity to support me and let the blood flow — from my feet to my heart.

It worked. I passed. Five years later, legs up the wall is still a trusted friend. My legs have felt the support of walls in hotels, in my closet, in my office, on retreats, in my bedroom, and probably a few other places I can't remember.

Putting my legs up the wall has the calming effect that I hear people talk about when using a weighted blanket, though I have never used one myself. All you need is a clear wall space! This shape calms your nervous system and mind, and, honestly, it feels delicious.

THE NUDGE

Start with a small space: a shelf, a corner of a desk,
a drawer, your kitchen counter, or that basket of folded and clean
laundry that has been sitting there for a week.

Set a timer for 5 minutes.
Focus on one thing at a time and decide where it belongs
(even if that is in the trash or recycle bin).

Sometimes I've been known to repeat
"I am creating space for what matters" or
"I am creating space for me to belong" as I go.

BE ROOTED #8

Declutter to make room for what matters.

I will never forget when one of my first coaches challenged me to an experiment. For an entire month, I wasn't "allowed" to take action on any of my ideas. The only "doing" I was allowed to do was to declutter. Big spaces. Little spaces. Any time an idea bubbled up, she encouraged me to write it down and then spend at least 5 minutes physically decluttering.

What happened in that month was more than cleaning my garage or desk. Every single time I physically decluttered even just a few minutes, my brain had its own metaphorical experience — as if sorting through the actual stuff allowed me to internally sort through all the emotions, thoughts, and ideas that mattered and release the ones that didn't.

Since then, decluttering is one of my personal go-to practices for getting rooted and allowing what is hidden and what matters to stand out — literally and figuratively.

Clutter builds up over time, which is why this is a powerful regular tending practice to help you get rooted in YOU.

One of my clients practices daily decluttering because she noticed that the act of putting things where they belong sends a message to her truest self that she is rooted in what matters most. Not only is her kitchen organized to start each day, but as she puts her dishes away, she invites her truest self to be seen, heard, and known.

This particular decluttering practice is less about how long you spend, or what you declutter, and more about the getting rooted in the process of discerning what matters, what doesn't, and allowing anything that is hidden to be seen.

THE NUDGE

Begin by noticing. Notice the words you are using toward yourself.

Perhaps you are a rockstar and have been filling up
on empowering language and thoughts.

Or perhaps the chorus sounds more like dismissiveness
or self-deprecating banter.

Maybe you notice that you use the word "just"
to describe your actions in a way that diminishes your value.
Or maybe you tell yourself that things aren't important
(which I'd invite you to consider is often code for
"I'm not important").

Once you've noticed your metaphorical rocks,
smile at yourself that you've noticed them.

And then decide: Could you replace one rock with a kinder,
more loving thought?

BE ROOTED #9
Tend to your roots.

The first step to planting a tree is to dig a hole. The second step, before anything gets planted, is all about tending.

I never realized how important this step was until I started doing more gardening in our new house — where the soil was a mixture of clay and rocks. So many rocks.

Just like plants prefer nutrient-rich soil rather than clay and rocks, it is important to take some time to tend to your "inner garden."

Consider the soil-tending metaphor. We want to plant seeds in soil that is fertile and loose, and maintains the right levels of moisture. The same holds true with our inner garden. We want to put our roots down in an inner garden that is loving, kind, and accepting.

The idea is that, before you can put down roots and rely on them to be strong, you need to tend to or nurture your inner resources with compassion and love.

THE NUDGE

Take a moment to pause and consider how you want to feel.

Notice what qualities or values will help you feel that way.

What matters to that version of you? What doesn't matter?

Knowing how you want to feel and what matters to you, imagine having an adult-sized bubble wand. (Remember the bubble wands we played with as kids? Magnify that by 10.)

See yourself blowing a bubble that grows so big that it surrounds you.

That bubble is filled with YOU. With the energy that you want to be ROOTED in. Outside that bubble is everything else.

Your bubble moves with you. And it is fluid. You can decide what is allowed INTO your bubble and what needs to stay out.

And because real life happens and sometimes our bubbles pop — you get to recreate your bubble whenever and wherever you need it.

Curious about the power of this nudge? I love how one of my clients, CIP, took this nudge and made it her own.

"When I find myself in a situation that starts to feel like angst or drama that may not have anything to do with me, I recall the energy hygiene trick that Elena added to my thriving arsenal.

Whether I visualize a forcefield, a shield, or Wonder Woman's bracelets, I let those unkind and/or unnecessary words or feelings bounce off my forcefield.

This trick also allows me to recognize that the person on the other side of the interaction is the one who needs compassion. I've even shared this "weapon of compassion" with several friends when I recognize that the words and actions of others are hurting them as well."

BE ROOTED #10
Tend to your energy hygiene.

Have you ever noticed that you feel pulled in all the directions?

That you want to say YES to prioritizing yourself but sometimes aren't sure how to do that? Or maybe that you find yourself getting sucked into other people's STUFF?

My clients often start their work with me unclear about their priorities. Or they think they know...but if they are being honest with themselves, their priorities feel more like shoulds than true desires.

Those shoulds are rooted in other people's truths. Expectations.

We are so very good at saying YES to others. At being people pleasers. But what if there was another way?

Saying no is a powerful practice. And necessary. But what if there was another boundary that mattered even more?

The thing about being rooted is that to truly say YES to you — you need boundaries. And not just boundaries about what you want to keep OUT. The way to stay rooted is to create boundaries that keep what MATTERS IN.

This nudge invites you to create boundaries that create space for YOU. For the things that make you YOU. For what matters to your truest self.

You can use it at the start of your day or before an event or meeting where you might normally go into people-pleasing mode.

THE NUDGE

The only thing you need is you.

Take a breath. Maybe another.

If you love ritual, you might pause and say hello
to your truest self. Maybe even express gratitude for their wisdom.

And then ask that truest version of you,
"What do I need to know today?"

Or, you can get specific if you are feeling particularly stuck on
one particular thing and ask, "What do I need to know about
_____ today?"

BE ROOTED #11

You have an inner guide.

Do you believe that you have an inner guide? A source of inner knowing?

Many of us have had moments of visceral knowing or a gut feeling. But more often than not, we don't trust those voices. Or we move so quickly through our lives, that we never stop to consider that we have a wellspring of guidance and knowledge within us.

One of the most powerful ways to get rooted is to connect with your inner guide. Because just like you know with certainty that the sun rises each day, you can be certain that you have an inner guide.

Your inner guide is your truest self. And that version of you knows exactly what you need and how to thrive and always has your back.

Many of us look for answers and clarity outside of ourselves. We forget that our very best teacher is always within us.

You probably are already on a first-name basis with your inner critic. I'd invite you to consider that your inner guide — or truest self — is a better companion.

This nudge is all about honoring your inner strength and wisdom and allowing it to not just exist but guide you.

Sometimes our inner wisdom is crystal clear. Sometimes it appears in the form of a sensation.

Sometimes the messages find you as you move through your day. I love to use this nudge at the start of my morning walks with my labradoodle, Jupiter. I allow my truest self and it's wisdom to find me through the creatures or nature that we encounter along the way.

THE NUDGE

Play with noticing where and how you can allow yourself
to belong...

First notice what belonging feels like to you?
Go back to a memory where you felt belonging.
What did that feel like? Look like? Sound like?

And then ask yourself:
What does my heart need for me to allow myself to belong?

What does my voice need?

What does my body need?

BE ROOTED #12
Allow yourself to belong.

I have a secret to tell you. I do not always feel like I belong.

And also? My belonging — or lack thereof — is an inside job.

Much of belonging questions lead back to my voice and my body, and my brain could write you a laundry list of all the times I didn't belong.

When my Italian cousins told me that I had an American accent when really I just wanted to be one of THEM.

When my second grade teacher told my parents I was too creative.

When a fifth grade girl sat atop a massive snowball on the playground and announced to me and the entire class that I had no friends.

But honestly, these aren't the moments that matter. The true not belonging was of my own doing. My own questioning. My doubt. My second-guessing. My hiding or playing small.

And just like I've had a tendency to limit my own belonging, I can also choose to ALLOW myself to belong.

Belonging starts within. And your roots...they grow stronger when they are allowed to belong.

This nudge is a reminder that the more you allow yourself to belong, the more rooted you are. It invites you to notice where you've put up walls or barriers that keep you from belonging. And to consider that there isn't a finish line or destination that reads "You belong." (Or maybe there is? Maybe that destination is in your HEART. Maybe that is the only finish line that matters?)

BE CURIOUS

Children are born curious.

They learn by exploring, by asking questions, and by allowing themselves to be drawn to things — just because. They don't censor themselves or wonder what other people might or might not think. But at some point, at least for many of us, that changes.

The change usually stems from pressure from well-meaning parents and a society that is steeped in judgment, expectations about what something SHOULD look like, needing to FIX or solve problems, and preferring certainty.

Do you remember the old-school MacGyver who could fix just about anything? (If you haven't seen the original, go search for it. You're welcome.)

While I appreciated MacGyver's ability to be creative, my hunch is that we spend a lot of our life trying to MacGyver our lives instead of truly living them.

What if there was another way? What if instead of always trying to IMPROVE or fix our lives, we could adopt curiosity as a mindset?

Full disclosure: Curiosity is one of my core values.

I've always been curious. As a child, I asked a lot of questions. So many questions that my parents sent me to the Encyclopedia Britannica anytime I had a question that could be researched, which led to mini projects on the Egyptian pyramids, cotton, and the state of New York.

Random, I know.

I can connect the dots between moments where I allowed myself to be curious and the most transformational experiences that have helped me inhabit my joy.

I went paragliding (and decided to embark on life coach training) because I was curious about the colorful parachutes coming down the mountain on our first day in Jackson Hole, Wyoming.

I decided that I wanted to learn to surf because I was curious about visiting a small village I'd heard so much about.

We built our new house because I followed the nudge of curiosity to spend an afternoon looking at model homes just for fun.

The power of these moments went beyond the short-term outcome of the experience.

The power of these moments is that they existed without any expectations. Without any shoulds. With sheer curiosity. With an open heart.

And each of them eventually became a domino that triggered an inner shift that helped me inhabit my joy and thrive as my truest self even more deeply.

Curiosity as a state of being is an act of self-love.

Being curious is compassionate. It invites you to be present to what is here for you.

It helps you inhabit your joy by nurturing and nourishing yourself instead of seeing yourself as someone that needs to be fixed.

Simply put: Expectations are a bundle of kryptonite and curiosity is the antidote.

When you are curious, you allow yourself to be whole. To connect to your senses, your instincts, your emotions, your rhythms, your desires, and your energy.

Let's get curious!

THE NUDGE

Give yourself 5 minutes to brainstorm: What are you curious about?

What are you feeling drawn to or intrigued by, just because?

The only rule to this brainstorm is not to censor yourself.
Let whatever bubbles up go onto your list.

And then, I invite you to notice any thoughts or judgments
that might come up.

They may or may not appear right away.
You might hear yourself saying things like:

Well yes, I'm curious, but I could never...

Or...This will never happen but...

Or...This is totally unlike me but...

All of those thoughts are worth noticing,
with one important caveat: I said notice, not judge.

As you observe the voices that emerge, you gain awareness.
And with awareness, you can get curious.

BE CURIOUS #1

What are you curious about?

A lot of us have picked up a nasty habit.

We've stopped listening to our instincts.

The truth is that not only are we not listening — we don't even create space for ourselves to notice our inner nudges because we prioritize what feels urgent in our day-to-day lives. So much so that the juicy deliciousness of our curiosity has gone dormant.

I remember working with one of my clients a few years ago, when I invited her to make a list of things she was curious about, just for fun.

This was HARD for her at first. She was so used to "doing" things out of habit and hadn't been tending to her curiosity muscle. But she kept going. And as she listed more things, it got easier to keep adding.

I asked her to consider which of the things on her list she could explore that day. Her first response was that she barely had time to take care of everything on her to-do list. She asked, "You aren't really suggesting I make time to research the bird I saw on my morning walk, are you?"

So I did what I do...and challenged her on the notion of not having time. She noticed that she had built a habit around telling herself what she did and didn't have time for. And that she'd fallen victim to prioritizing productivity.

She is not alone in prioritizing what is urgent. Or having stories that keep her on autopilot. Maybe you do that too?

This nudge is less about DOING anything and more about rebuilding your curiosity muscle. You might find that the more you play with the practice, the more you'll find ways to nurture and then nourish your curiosity.

THE NUDGE

Notice: Is there something you are trying to FIX or change?
In your life? In your body? In your career? In your relationships?

Pick one thing that you've been actively trying to "fix."
Consider the question: Why?
Why do you want to fix or change this?

And then consider how you might treat yourself
if you believed there was nothing to fix.
If you treated yourself like your own BFF?
If you offered yourself tenderness, nurturing, or self-compassion?

BE CURIOUS #2

What are you trying to fix?

I have a question for you: When was the last time you weren't trying to FIX something about yourself? Or your life?

What if you could stop trying to fix everything? No, really. Pause for a moment. Consider.

This might sound scary. I get it. We are programmed to fix. To strive. To want to improve. And, yes, there are times to fix.

I'm proposing that we flip the equation and lead with curiosity and love rather than fixing as our go-to operating system for thriving.

I'm in the business of transformation...so this might sound strange. But I have news for you: You don't need to be fixed. It is as simple as that.

I spent a lot of my life chasing goals. I guess it goes with the territory as a cancer survivor who always felt like she had something to prove, until the day that I realized that maybe there was another way.

Fixing assumes brokenness. It comes from a place of not enough. And more often than not, the fixing comes with a lot of force and effort.

By all means, put the band-aid on when you are bleeding – but consider what would happen if the next time life showed up with a challenge, you could get curious about how to offer yourself compassion instead of judgment.

THE NUDGE

Take a moment right now.

Maybe take a breath.

And then ask yourself the question:

What would feel like delight today?

BE CURIOUS #3

What would feel like delight today?

Delight is everywhere.

But in a world where we scan through our surroundings and days like we scan our social media feeds, our ability to recognize delight gets lost in the sea of judgment and overthinking.

This nudge is an invitation to connect to delight as a navigational tool.

I once heard a podcast host encourage the audience to use the feeling of LOVE as a guide for making decisions. His nudge was to, during uncertain or challenging moments, ask the question, What would LOVE do in this moment?

I loved that. But I love it even more with delight as the filter.

The thing about delight is that it is personal to you. And...your answer to what would feel like delight might change on any given day as a barometer of your aliveness.

Maybe instead of dreading sitting in traffic, I could connect to what feels like delight by playing a favorite song and singing out loud — or call a friend that I haven't chatted with in a while.

Or maybe instead of feeling like I don't have any time on a busy day, I could take a quick moment in between Zoom calls to look at my plant cuttings and notice the new roots that are growing.

This nudge isn't a magic eraser. But it reminds us that we can use curiosity as a tool to inhabit our joy in the little moments. And it might just create small windows or doors in what originally felt like big brick walls of over-thinking.

THE NUDGE

This practice invites you to be a detective.
To notice. You are simply gathering information.

You can set an alarm on your phone or put these two- to three-
minute check-ins into your schedule or connect them
to a habit that you already have (like sitting down at your desk
or washing your hands).

Notice and consider:

What physical sensations do I feel in my body in this moment?

What is my brain thinking about in this moment?

What emotions am I feeling in this moment?

BE CURIOUS #4

Explore your inner landscape.

*"We ought to view ourselves with the same curiosity and openness
with which we study a tree, the sky, or a thought,
because we too are linked to the entire universe."*

HENRI MATISSE

So often we think of curiosity as something that is outward. And sometimes it is.

But for today I'm inviting you to explore your inner landscape without judgment. Without needing to DO anything.

To simply notice and be curious about how you feel. About the sensations and emotions that you experience. To allow and observe your thoughts.

The truth is that those sensations, those thoughts, or those emotions are actually benevolent messengers. They are nudges asking you to pay attention rather than ignore or bull-doze your way through all the things.

This nudge invites you to be an observer of the benevolent messages that your mind, body, and soul are trying to send you.

While it might feel strange to observe and not DO, this exploration is based on the idea that becoming present, aware, and connected to yourself is at the very core of being curious in other aspects of your life.

THE NUDGE

The next time you feel stuck or indecisive and hear yourself saying (or thinking) "I don't know"...take a breath.

And then consider:

What would you do or who would you BE if you DID know?

Because the truth is that most of the time, you cannot get it wrong.
I promise.

BE CURIOUS #5

What if you did know?

"I don't know isn't an answer."

I remember my mom saying this to me as a child. (Or at least I think I remember. I can't really say, "I don't know how it started...") :)

And now, as a coach, it isn't a phrase that I allow my clients to answer with. Ok, that sounds harsh. They are allowed to answer in whatever way they'd like, but I usually follow up with this nudge: What if you did know?

"I don't know" is an easy answer. It is a safe space to be. It prolongs not having to take action or move toward what matters most. And it is a method of self-sabotage.

Because here is the thing: "I don't know" is a habit. It is a trap. It erodes your curiosity. It is like a brick wall that keeps you from possibility and thriving.

"I don't know" comes from wanting to get things right. Wanting to avoid the F-word (not that F-word). I'm talking about failure. But there is no such thing as failure.

There is experimentation. There is feedback. There is learning.

You don't have to know the details or specifics. You only need to open the door to possibility with a dose of curiosity.

THE NUDGE

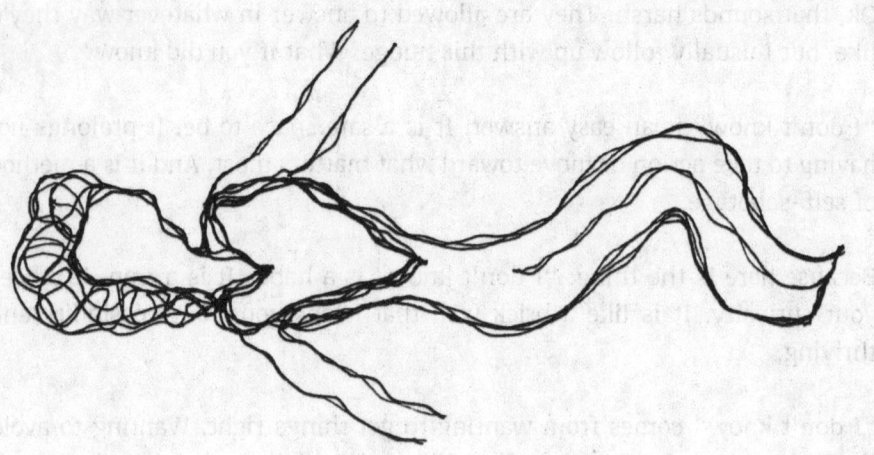

Find a guide to the yin yoga shapes on page 95

BE CURIOUS #6
Take a supine twist.

Hang out with any life coach or yoga teacher and you'll hear the invitation to release what no longer serves you.

(Yes, this includes me. I've offered it many, many times.)

But at some point, I realized that in order to release whatever it is...we first have to get to know what it is we are holding on to.

I know we'd like to flip a switch and easily let go of all stuff...but as Pema Chödrön says, "Nothing ever goes away until it has taught us what we need to know."

One of my favorite places to connect to whatever I'm holding on to is in the body. And in particular laying down on my back in a delicious twist.

Twists are juicy for so many reasons, including improving digestion and creating ease. And they are a fabulous place to get curious about whatever your body, mind, or heart are holding on to.

Add in the deliciousness of your breath and the support of gravity in this shape and you may find yourself lingering here to just BE.

THE NUDGE

Grab a piece of paper or journal.

Ask yourself: What is working? What is going right?
What progress can I celebrate?

(No, you don't need to ask yourself all three. Usually one of those
phrases will resonate more than another on any given day.)

This nudge is great anytime you want to check in with yourself.
And while you can do it without writing it down, I find that our brain
tends to forget what is working when left to its own devices.
Writing it down serves to track your noticings as evidence and helps
you integrate this practice.

BE CURIOUS #7
What is working?

I've always been a silver lining girl. I can find the celebration or progress in just about anything.

I've also never really been a fan of unlimited venting sessions about all the things that are going wrong. Yes, we all need to vent...but we all have that person in our lives that only ever talks about all the things that are bad or wrong. If I'm being honest, that energy exhausts me.

We are excellent at noticing all the things that are going WRONG.

And yet...getting curious about noticing what's working creates a powerful energetic shift.

This particular nudge is the one that my clients love to hate. They know that it is the first question I'll ask when we start talking.

Some of them plan for that. Others still try to start with what isn't working, which I love. Because inevitably, they will have shared someTHING that was working. Some progress that they were diminishing or dismissing — they just couldn't see it.

This nudge takes PRACTICE. It requires effort to get curious, notice, and allow. It invites you to be present. It doesn't mean that everything is rainbows and unicorns, but it fills you up on the good stuff. We need the good stuff, just like your phone needs to be charged or your body needs food as fuel.

If you believe that what you focus on is what grows, this nudge helps you grow a garden of noticing progress and celebrating even the smallest of moments.

THE NUDGE

Go for a curiosity scavenger hunt.

Choose a day or a part of it, intentionally — to inspire your curiosity and let it emerge from within you.

And then, pick something — or a time in your day — that feels ripe with possibility.

It could be taking a right instead of a left on your way to work or while you run errands (or walk your dog).

It could be reading a new book or listening to a new podcast.

Maybe spend time looking out a window or walking in nature.

Maybe you decide to doodle or color or sing or dance out loud.

The "what" doesn't actually matter. What matters is the purposeful cultivating and then receiving of curiosity.

BE CURIOUS #8

Go on a curiosity scavenger hunt.

Most of us move FAST through our day. We fill up on productivity and doing.

While that might be good for your to-do list, it doesn't necessarily help you with getting curious.

What I know to be true is that curiosity meets you where you are, literally and figuratively. Or at least it does...if you allow it to.

Curiosity can find me when I'm lying in bed, during a Peloton ride, in the middle of the shower...and occasionally while sitting at my desk. But there are also certain moments and experiences that help inspire and amplify my curiosity.

Being in nature makes me curious. I notice new sounds, am more apt to explore an unknown path, or wonder what animal made specific tracks.

Reading books, listening to podcasts, and listening to NPR often lead me to want to learn more about a topic or person.

Meditation reveals enough stillness that I can notice messages in my heart that I might otherwise miss.

Going for a walk or practicing yoga helps me consider new perspectives that I've never thought of and lead me to wonder about possibilities I might never have imagined.

This nudge reminds you that inspiration is everywhere.

I love this practice because it reminds us to find wonder in not just the big, obvious experiences but also the smallest of things. It invites you to let your heart be stirred or touched by something that catches your interest, for whatever reason.

THE NUDGE

Try adding an AND in to replace the all-or-nothing thinking.

This practice doesn't change the circumstances,
but it creates an energetic shift that reminds the brain that your
thriving isn't defined by one moment.

BE CURIOUS #9

Create space for AND instead of OR.

I want you to be able to not just withstand but thrive through the ups and downs of life.

I spent a lot of my life in an all-or-nothing approach. All in for my goals. All in for my habits. Feeling good when I was on target. Feeling bad when I was off track.

Feeling swept up by others or defined by the turbulence of life instead of what was working.

Inhabiting your joy isn't about ignoring intensity or challenge. But it does ask you to get curious about the AND.

Have you ever had a moment where something was HARD and you felt proud of yourself at the same time? Or that you were sad and grateful at the same time?

So many of us live in the all or nothing. We've fallen into a pattern of dismissing our thriving when something happens that makes things feel topsy-turvy.

Maybe you can relate?

I want you to know that there isn't a "non-compete" clause when it comes to your thriving. You can thrive even when things feel challenging.

You can thrive and inhabit your joy even when life is stormy.

You aren't defined by your up moments. Or your down moments.

You thrive in the AND moments.

THE NUDGE

What are you ready to illuminate?
What would it take to give yourself permission
to be your own light?

BE CURIOUS #10

What are you ready to illuminate?

I crave light. I love sunshine and sunrise in particular — watching light grow in all directions. I'm the person who turns all the lights on in any room I'm in and chooses hotel rooms based on their windows.

And yet, over the years, I've learned something.

Years ago, my husband and I sat on the beach, overlooking Banderas Bay in Nuevo Vallarta, Mexico. The bright (almost blinding) sun gave way to dark storm clouds in the distance. Clouds that loomed with power. Clouds that banded together to create a mass of energy. I was transfixed. In awe.

I watched with curiosity. It was hard not to notice the dark mass that had formed, creating a bridge from the sky to sea. Would it move towards us? Would it unleash a torrent of rain upon us?

Eventually, it did what storms do. It moved. It rained. And then the clouds began to give way. They didn't disappear entirely, but they shifted. In those shifts, cracks of light began to shine though. First small ones. Then bigger ones that revealed patches of blue sky playing peekaboo.

In that moment, I remembered: Illumination exists everywhere. Even in darkness. And, more importantly, darkness offers the potential for light.

Darkness is not the opposite of light. It is energy, waiting to be revealed. Sometimes as a storm of torrential forces and sometimes as subtle shifts that reveal a radiant shine.

Too often we let ourselves get bogged down by darkness.

What if instead of wishing it away, we could get curious and observe it? Be open to the potential energy that it could offer? What if you could believe that you make your own light? What if you could be your own light?

BE ALIVE

"I don't want to get to the end of my life and find that I have
just lived the length of it. I want to have lived the width of it as well."

DIANE ACKERMAN

I remember the gut-punch I felt when I first read these words.

I spent a lot of my life in survival mode, aka "the length." I was a do-er. I was a survivor. I was also numb. And on most days, I functioned more like a bull-dozer than fully alive to the experience.

But the more I got rooted and curious, the more I realized aliveness is mine to tap into, EVERY. SINGLE. DAY.

Aliveness is an invitation to live the FULL experience of life. Being alive is about being present, connected, and AWAKE in your life.

I thought I knew what aliveness looked and felt like, but in the summer of 2021 I traveled to Costa Rica with my husband. What I experienced was the ultimate masterclass in all things aliveness.

I'd heard about the famous saying "Pura Vida"...but seeing "Pure Life" come alive around me, lit me up from the inside out.

Sloths, monkeys, spiders, and birds. Plants and flowers of every color possible bursting with vibrancy. The orchids that grow on the trunks of trees. The cactus that stood strong on the shore of the ocean. The rain. The sun. The vibrancy of the jungle. The interconnectedness of the mangroves. The people who are fully present.

Getting alive is about claiming and owning your joy instead of outsourcing it to others.

Getting alive in your life isn't a destination. It is an ongoing process of embodiment. It allows. It celebrates. It feels. It ebbs and flows in contradictions.

Simply put: The more alive you are, the more you thrive. And the more you thrive, the more you can inhabit your joy.

Let's get alive!

THE NUDGE

Find a song you love.

Turn it on.

And dance.

BE ALIVE #1
Take a dance break.

I've never considered myself a good dancer. And yet, some of the moments where I could literally feel the pulse of my heart and the energy of life moving through me happened while dancing.

I'm not talking about structured dance. (In fact, the one time I tried swing dancing lessons I had my first ever panic attack. It wasn't pretty.)

I'm talking about allowing the music to move YOU.

Allowing your body to embody the feel of the music and express itself through movement.

I became a fan of taking dance breaks once I started working from home, but real talk: I didn't prioritize it.

That changed when I experienced Body Groove with master teacher Heather Winia. I want you to imagine dance meets yoga meets your five-year-old self skipping at a playground.

The freedom that I felt flowing through my veins was an instant jolt of aliveness. And my mind? My heart wasn't judging or second-guessing. I wasn't overthinking or constraining myself.

Since then, I've taken to dancing in my office, in my closet, and around my kitchen with my teenager (sometimes it is me dancing and her laughing at me). Sometimes I sing out loud. Sometimes I close my eyes. There isn't a wrong way to do this.

The power of a dance break is in allowing yourself to be fully present with the music and allow your aliveness to...come alive.

THE NUDGE

Find a guide to the yin yoga shapes on page 95

BE ALIVE #2

Pour gratitude into your heart.

We hear a lot about gratitude as a powerful practice for good reason. Gratitude is an invitation to be truly present in your life, with what you appreciate. With what fills you. With what you love.

The more present you are in your aliveness, the more you will notice gratitude. And the more you fill up with gratitude, the more alive you feel.

There are a lot of gratitude practices out there. Which is why I'd like to offer a different way to truly feel your gratitude and let it fill you.

It starts in your body with what is known in yoga as a supported bridge.

This shape invites you to imagine that you are pouring gratitude from your hips and belly into your heart.

Can you fill up on gratitude without getting down on the floor and moving into a supported bridge? Yes.

But there is something so juicy about feeling your feet, your tailbone, and the back of your skull supported by the earth and allowing your gratitude to flow up from your feet, into your legs, hips, belly and all the way to your heart.

The longer you stay, the more your heart can expand — and overflow — with your gratitude.

THE NUDGE

Write yourself a love letter. Or decide to write yourself
(daily? weekly?) love notes.

The "what" of what you write isn't important.
These can be messages of inspiration, compassion,
or reminders about what truly matters (or doesn't).

BE ALIVE #3

Write yourself a love letter.

I loved getting notes in middle and high school. This probably isn't a thing anymore, but back then, I remember long and short notes folded into rectangles that could fit in the palm of your hand to be passed from desk to desk without the teacher noticing. (The teachers, by the way, always noticed. Even when they didn't show it.)

Granted, some notes were not always kind. And I'm pretty sure that some boy broke up with me via note. But for the most part, these small bundles were full of goodness and delight.

Fast forward to all these years later, I'm a believer in tending your aliveness by giving yourself what you crave. One of the ways to do that is to write yourself a love letter.

I invited one of my Thrive Unleashed clients, Karen, to create her own love letter practice. She made it her own by deciding to end her day with a short phrase or a word "love note" to herself and place it in a tin.

Here is what happened for Karen:

"In adopting this nudge, I end my day with a positive feeling about myself. On days that may be harder I can go back to my tin and pull out some much needed love from me to myself and it instantly connects me to being alive, brightens my mindset and internal peace. The other magical piece of this practice is reinforcing my truths that I have suppressed or put aside while focusing on all the other things in my world. Watching it fill with joyous thoughts about myself has been amazingly powerful and I love ending the day filling my jar of positivity."

THE NUDGE

Ask yourself: How do I want to feel?

You can ask yourself this while brushing your teeth in the morning. Or before going into a meeting. You can ask it when starting a new project or planning a trip, or even prior to a workout or phone call.

Once you know how you want to feel, you can think of your intention as something to tend to and cultivate. As something you need to get to know and build a relationship with.

Does it have a color? A word (or song) that goes along with it? Is there an image or symbol that might represent the feeling? And what does that feeling feel like in your body?

And most importantly: Consider where this feeling already exists in your life today. And how might you bring that feeling to life right now?

BE ALIVE #4

How do you want to feel?

I spent most of my life being a goal setter. There was always a goal I was working toward.

But at some point I realized that more than being a goal setter, I was a perpetually unsatisfied goal setter.

For every outcome I'd been seeking, there was a string of judgments about how it wasn't enough. Or I could have done better. Or...the noticing that it didn't feel as good as I thought it might (or "should").

Can you relate?

Everything shifted when I realized that owning my joy — truly inhabiting it — meant not waiting for the finish line or end goal to feel how I wanted to feel.

Are end goals or finish lines important? Yes. But what if they aren't the ultimate metric of your thriving? What if your thriving and inhabiting your joy happened in the process...along the way?

What I came to understand was that the power was in tending to my intention...the way I wanted to FEEL. Not just at the end. Not just when I submitted the THING, learned to do X, lost 10 pounds, or literally crossed the finish line of a race.

An intention is a desire to feel a certain way. A desire to BE a certain way. And your intention is something that you can connect to — and cultivate — every single day as a way to allow your ALIVENESS to grow.

It all starts with one question: How do you want to feel?

Once you know how you want to feel, you can cultivate attunement to that feeling and let the BEING direct the DOING.

THE NUDGE

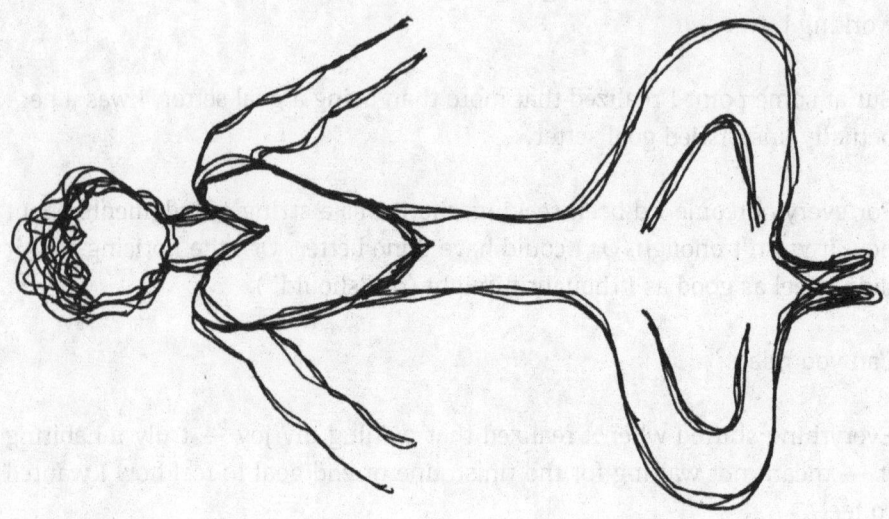

Move yourself into a reclined bound angle shape on a yoga mat,
blanket, or even lying in bed. Place your right hand on your belly and
your left hand on your heart.

Breathe. In and out.

And ask your heart: What am I ready to open up to?

Receive whatever is there for you. Be with it without judgment.

Find a guide to the yin yoga shapes on page 95

BE ALIVE #5

What can you open your heart to?

Do you ever limit how good you feel? Or perhaps there are limits to how much you can let yourself feel?

Aliveness is a practice of allowing. Of allowing your heart to be stirred. Of allowing yourself to RECEIVE and savor the life that you've created for yourself.

Real talk: We aren't always good at receiving. And we are even worse at steeping in the good stuff.

What if you could expand your capacity by allowing yourself to connect to your aliveness — and whatever it is you want to cultivate?

What if all it took was opening your heart?

I get it. A lot of us keep our hearts well-protected. Because feeling the feels can be HARD.

But there is another way. A way to allow yourself to feel your aliveness. And it starts in your body.

Reclined bound angle pose is a shape that invites allowing. It asks you to open yourself up — literally and figuratively — to receive and BE with whatever is here for you.

THE NUDGE

Take a moment to reflect: What unexpected moment
of delight can you savor from your day?

BE ALIVE #6

Savor unexpected delight.

*"Something important is always about to happen, my dear girl.
And if not, you'd do well to act as if it were. You'll enjoy life better that way."*

—Lady Danbury in *It's in His Kiss* by Julia Quinn

I'm a chaser of delight. Big delight and little delight. It fills me.

And yet I realized something a few years ago. I spent a lot of my life trying to plan, control, and manage my delight.

The problem with that is that the best delight or the truest delights aren't things you can plan for.

Delight is spontaneous. It exists in unexpected moments.

What would your day be like if you allowed in more unexpected delight?

If you noticed moments of wonder instead of judgment? Honored delight instead of guilt?

Unexpected delight is available to you every day in the big and little moments. It is a condition of aliveness. Of allowing the ordinary moments of day-to-day life to touch you.

The colors of wildflowers along the highway. The song that comes on the radio that reminds you of a moment you'd forgotten. A butterfly that lands on a plant outside your window. The scent of a favorite food or the feeling of warmth from your coffee cup in your hands.

This nudge is about collecting evidence of delight as a metric of your aliveness and your thriving (instead of all the things that didn't go as planned).

THE NUDGE

What have you been putting off in your life?

Make a list of all the things you've been putting off
or procrastinating on because now isn't the right time.

If you aren't sure where to start, think back to conversations or
daydreams where you've said things like:

That would be fabulous, but I can't possibly _____ .

I know what I need to do for _____ ,
but I'm just too busy right now.

When I retire, I'll _____ .

I'll do _____ when I've lost these last 10 pounds.

I just need to _____ before I can _____ .

The second step is...(here comes the courage part!)...pick one
of the things. Let it be scary. It might even feel slightly nauseating.
Or maybe it feels small but powerful. The "what" doesn't matter.

Once you've picked your thing, consider these questions:

1. Why is this important?
2. What will change in your life if you bring it to life?
3. How will it FEEL to bring this forward?
4. What would you need to let go of to take a step toward this
   FEELING if you weren't worried about the outcome? (Notice
   this is about the feeling, not the outcome.)
5. What would you need to believe to step toward this feeling?

And then...what is one seed that you can plant today? And what will it
look like to cultivate that seed and allow it to grow?

BE ALIVE #7

Stop waiting for the right conditions.

Many of us are skilled waiters. We wait for the perfect conditions. For all the details to be fully fleshed out. In a way, we procrastinate our joy. Our aliveness.

Here is the thing: Your conditions are holding you hostage.

And I get it. We are afraid of what-ifs. We don't love uncertainty.

But those what-ifs are keeping you out of your aliveness. That waiting is a form of outsourcing your joy instead of owning it right now.

I remember when I started thinking about leaving my career as a teacher.

The conditions were far from perfect. I didn't have a solid plan to replace that income. It felt irresponsible to leave a thing that I was good at for a dream.

There was so much I didn't know. But the idea of staying felt like golden handcuffs.

You've put so much on hold because now isn't a good time.

And, no, the road ahead may not be easy.

But it does start with a decision to give yourself permission to own your own joy.

When you inhabit your joy, you stop waiting for the perfect conditions and allow yourself to name, claim, and OWN what it is that is truly important and what you want — right now.

THE NUDGE

Create your own hot damn experiment moment by saying "hot damn" before you start a project, meeting, workout, or conversation.

Explore, be curious, and connect to the inner strength and wisdom that is already within you.

Notice how you feel and what emerges.

You might just realize that you can look at yourself, your life, and your dreams and realize, "Hot damn, I created this."

BE ALIVE #8

A hot damn experiment.

You already know that what you put your attention on is what you notice more of. So it makes sense that the right words can help you create energetic shifts when you need them.

Think about it. There are probably certain words that you use or phrases that make you feel something. That connects you to a certain energy or emotion.

I stumbled upon one of those phrases for myself during the latter part of 2020, after the initial months of the pandemic and what we were all facing started to feel even more real. I needed a kickstart to keep showing up for myself, for my work, and for the potential that I knew was inside me.

I was craving something audacious to help me up-level my aliveness and thriving.

I found that energy in the words "hot damn."

The truth is that it isn't really the words that matter. The energy that you crave is already inside you. But sometimes we need a nudge to help draw that energy out. To allow it to come to life within us.

So I went on a hot damn experiment. Every time I sat down to work, got ready for a meeting, prepared to have what might be a challenging conversation — and sometimes even before a workout — I said "hot damn."

The more I practiced, the more I inhabited the feeling.

With each "hot damn," I allowed myself to show up a bit more courageously. As I continued, I realized that not only did I have nothing to lose by showing up in my life as my truest self — I had everything to GAIN.

THE NUDGE

Get your pen and paper ready.

Name three things that you NEED today, this week, or this month.

And then name three things you WANT today,
this week, or this month.

Choose one thing from each of your lists and consider:

Why is that thing important to you? In your life?

Who might you be able to ask for help toward that need or want?

And then...do the thing.

Make the ask.

Allow it to be THAT easy.

Side note: This is less about actually getting the THING
(though that is fabulous too!) and more about getting connected
with your needs, your wants, and your DESIRES.

BE ALIVE #9

Ask for what you need (and want!).

What would be different in your life if you believed you could have what you needed? What you wanted? Without guilt?

Let me first acknowledge the elephant in the room. You might be out of practice in naming your wants and needs. Am I right?

We've prioritized tending to the wants and needs of others for such a long time, we've stopped listening to the voice of our own desires. Or we feel guilty about wanting. (And asking? Gah.)

What if your aliveness depended on you naming, claiming, and owning your needs and wants?

Despite what your brain might think, allowing the people in your life that love you the most to support and help you is a gift you can give them.

I spent years believing I needed to do everything myself as a result of both surviving cancer and then getting divorced. My brain told me that my success relied on me being totally independent and self-sufficient. But I realized there was another way.

Asking for help and naming my desires and my needs wasn't me being selfish. My husband LOVES when I get specific about what I need and allow him to help me. (Ok, maybe he doesn't LOVE all of my requests. Like walking the dog in the middle of the night.) The better I've gotten about asking for help, the more our relationship has improved.

We spend so much time making assumptions, overthinking, and judging our needs. But the more fluent you are with naming your desires, the easier they flow.

You might even catch yourself thinking, "Wait? Can it be THIS easy?" The answer is YES, it can.

THE NUDGE

Notice:

Where are expectations making you grippy?

Where are you holding on to what something has to look like
to be "a success?"

What might it be like to soften that grip?
What might you need to believe?

And then decide:

What are you committed to? Why?

And how might you get curious about creating a ripple of energy
toward that desire?

And then what is one small ripple-creating action that you can take
TODAY to set that intention in motion?

BE ALIVE #10

Determination without expectation.

Expectations are pure kryptonite.

I know this because I spent a lot of my life attached to outcomes. Until the day that I literally belly-flopped off a surfboard.

Years ago, I found myself noticing the look of pride on the face of a young girl taking surf lessons. Her energy as she rode a wave to shore was contagious, and I wanted to feel it too.

So I set out to find a way. To go all in.

Except that I was in tears after the first two days of a surf and yoga retreat – and never standing up on the board "successfully." It was at that moment that our instructor, Nic, said the magic words to me:

"What if you practiced determination instead of expectation? What if you could be determined to make progress, but let go of what you expect it to look like?"

He pointed out that I was actually a very strong paddler. And I WAS sensing the waves and then riding them, even if on my belly. But because I was so hell-bent on what I thought it had to look like, I hadn't given myself credit for what was working.

I went back into the water as a different woman on the third day. And guess what? I did stand. (Only for a moment, because at that moment I was in shock — and proceeded to epic belly flop into the water in sheer delight.)

The shift between determination and expectation happens when you explore how to cultivate attunement rather than attainment.

Because getting grippy takes us AWAY from our intentions. And determination — and intention — take you toward your JOY.

THE NUDGE

How might you connect to your inner aliveness
through creativity TODAY?

Without overthinking it, choose one way to cultivate
your creativity even for just 5 minutes. Need some ideas?
Go back to what you explored in your scavenger hunt and
get creative with something you found.

BE ALIVE #11
Cultivate creativity.

When was the last time you nurtured or tended to your creativity? Too often as adults, we ignore our creativity.

We tell ourselves that we don't have time for it. We aren't "good at it."

We put the creativity of others on a pedestal, as a finished product.

We judge. We label. We compare.

But what if there was another way?

What if we approached creativity as instinctive?

As something that is available to all of us? As something you can nurture and tend to?

Maybe you draw. Maybe you sing. Maybe you knit. Maybe you doodle in the margin of this book. Maybe you write or play an instrument. Maybe you arrange flowers or paint. Maybe you create a new recipe.

This nudge isn't about the finished product. It comes alive when you show up for the process.

What if cultivating your creativity was more than something you do once in a blue moon when you go to the wine and painting place with a group of friends?

THE NUDGE

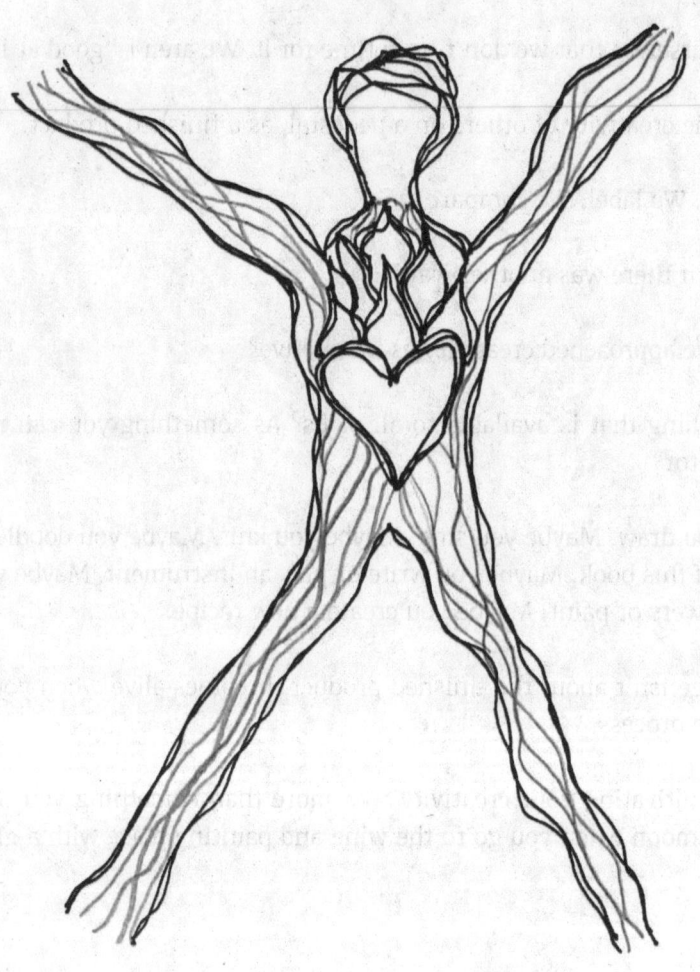

Find a guide to the yin yoga shapes on page 95

BE ALIVE #12

Open your wings.

Your body knows things long before your mind does. I believe this down to my core. Your body is your connection to your aliveness. Not just when you are dancing or getting your heart pumping.

I remember studying to be a yoga teacher in 2016 and practicing cueing a breath-to-movement sequence that included what is known as "star pose." As I practiced feeling this shape of arms extended and heart open in my body, something shifted inside me.

Three breaths into the shape, I found that I couldn't help myself from smiling.

Psychologists like Amy Cuddy have studied how the position of our bodies impacts our emotions and how we feel about ourselves. But I didn't need to read the research to understand what I was feeling. I felt alive. Like I could do anything.

I even started labeling this shape as the one that could "make even my grumpy teenager smile" after inviting my daughter to try the pose and watching her mood shift every single time.

Extending my arms out is still my favorite shape when I want to take in an experience. It reminds me of a mythical creature opening its wings to receive.

This nudge is about allowing your body to be a doorway. Into your aliveness. Into your power. Into truly inhabiting your joy.

The beauty of taking a moment (or two or three) in a star pose is that you can do it ANYWHERE. In your closet. On a mountaintop or beach. In your office. In the bathroom. The only thing you need is you.

THE NUDGE

Where have you been afraid to get breathless?

Where have you been choosing the "easy" path?

And how might you allow yourself to get breathless today?

BE ALIVE #13

Allow yourself to be breathless.

When was the last time you were breathless?

What I know about being breathless is that we tend to see it as a sign of weakness. A sign of struggle.

What if there was a different perspective?

I first remember noticing my breathlessness on a hiking retreat. The longer and faster we hiked, the louder my breath got. And the louder it sounded in my brain, the more my inner critic had to say.

I told myself that I was weak. That my oncologist was right all those years ago when he'd explained my chemotherapy induced lung damage. I remember sitting in front of Kirkland, the retreat director, when I told him that I thought I should move to a slower-paced group. Tears started to fall as I doubted whether or not I could keep up.

Kirkland listened. And then he invited me to consider that maybe the others in my group were breathing heavily as well. That maybe being short of breath simply meant that I was doing something that was challenging. And that being challenged might be a good thing.

Yes, I could move to a different pace group — and perhaps breathe easier. Or maybe I could give myself and my breath permission to be stronger than I thought. (Yes, I stayed. Yes, my breath was still loud. And I kept going anyway.)

Giving ourselves permission to be breathless isn't just about our lungs.

Being breathless is about expanding our capacity. It represents a yearning so strong that we allow ourselves to go ALL in. To challenge our comfort zone.

And what if the practice of getting to the point of breathlessness was actually an invitation to create ease, even during a challenge?

THE NUDGE

Pause for a moment. Take a breath, in and out.

Ask yourself: What would feel delicious today? (Or in this moment?)

Allow your heart to answer the question. And know that the answer almost doesn't matter. Maybe you can bring it forward or maybe you can't. But notice how you feel when you ask yourself the question and allow an answer to bubble up inside you.

BE ALIVE #14

What would feel delicious?

I have a favorite question that I love to ask myself. A question that is a game-changer for cultivating the quality of life that you want to feel more of any given day.

And although I've loved it for a while, it became one of my go-to tending practices during the pandemic.

There I was, on a random morning in February 2020. I was used to working from home prior to all things COVID, but I was tired. Tired of uncertainty. Tired of overthinking.

I remember getting ready for the day, pulling out another pair of yoga pants and a Zoom-ready top...when I paused. My favorite question whispered it-self to me.

"What would feel delicious?"

My answer came out of nowhere. Ok, that isn't true. The answer came from deep within me.

The answer led me to open my jewelry drawer and pick up the red velvet pouch that had previously sat unopened for a very long time. A pouch that contained my great-grandmother's pearls.

As I put them on my neck, I heard my mom's voice when I was younger tell-ing me that pearls needed to be worn to maintain their shine. As I closed the clasp, my heart smiled. I'd asked a question and my inner teacher's answer connected me back to generations of strong women — from my great-grand-mother to my grandmothers, to my mom — and to my aliveness.

This nudge connects you with what lights you up so that you can inhabit your joy on any given day. It offers you a way to be curious and invites you to gift yourself self-love.

RESOURCES

A GUIDE TO THE YIN YOGA SHAPES

*For guided practices through each shape, visit: www.elenasonnino.com/inhab-it-your-joy

These shapes can be practiced on a yoga mat, a carpet, or even on your bed. You can make them extra delicious with a pillow or a blanket. (Or both.)

CHILD'S POSE

Find a comfortable spot on the floor with a yoga mat, carpet, or blanket.

Begin in a kneeling position.

Allow your knees to widen and your big toes to touch as you invite your hips to move toward your heels. You can use a pillow or blanket under the hips to feel more supported.

Slowly guide your torso down toward the ground so that your forehead is supported by the earth (or another pillow or blanket).

Your arms can reach forward or toward your ankles.

Stay here for up to 10 minutes.

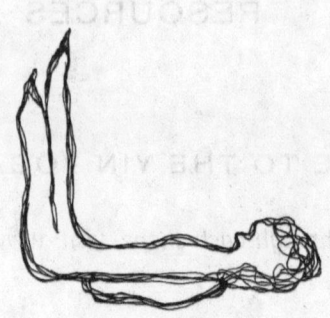

LEGS UP THE WALL

You'll want an open wall space or the back of a couch for this shape.

Place your mat or a blanket perpendicular to the wall and then scoot yourself up to sit with one of your hips up against the wall.

Swing your legs up to the wall as the rest of your body moves down to the floor.

From here, scoot yourself closer to the wall so that the backs of your legs are supported by the wall.

Explore where your arms feel most at ease (by your side, with your hands on your belly, or reaching behind you).

It can feel extra delicious to place a blanket or pillow underneath your hips.

Stay here for 5-20 minutes.

This is an inversion and is contra-indicated if you have uncontrolled high blood pressure, glaucoma, or have neck issues.

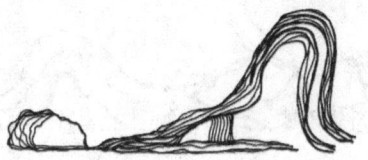

SUPPORTED BRIDGE

Begin on your back on either a yoga mat or a carpet. Have a blanket or a pillow close by.

Notice the ground as it supports the back side of your body.

Guide your feet to the mat so that the soles of your feet are on the ground and walk your heels toward your hips.

Gently lift your hips just enough to place the pillow or blanket underneath your tailbone (where you'd normally have a label on your jeans). Allow your tailbone to feel supported.

Your arms can rest by your sides.

Stay here for 5-20 minutes.

This is an inversion and is contra-indicated if you have uncontrolled high blood pressure, glaucoma, or have neck or disc issues.

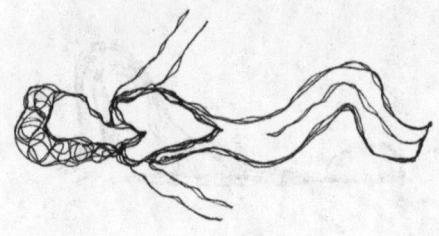

SUPINE TWISTS

Begin by lying down on your mat or on a comfortable carpet. Have a blanket or pillow available.

Gently hug your right knee in toward your chest. Stay there for a few rounds of breath.

Slowly guide your right knee across your body, to the left, as your right arm extends out from your shoulder. You can support your right knee (and bring the earth closer to you) with the blanket or pillow or allow gravity to guide you.

Give yourself permission to come out of the twist a bit if you notice that your right shoulder is off the ground. Breathe.

Stay on this side for 5-10 minutes and then slowly guide the knee back to center. Extend the right leg all the way out and notice how the body feels. Repeat on the other side when you are ready.

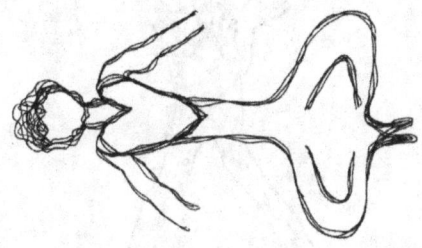

RECLINED BOUND ANGLE

Begin in a comfortable seated position. Have two blankets or pillows close by.

Allow the soles of your feet to come together (your knees will go wide). Allow your feet to move away from the pelvis if you notice that the knees are high off the ground.

From there, lower your torso down to the ground. If the knees are still off the ground, place a blanket or pillow underneath the knees or thighs.

Allow your head, neck, and spine to feel supported.

Bring your right hand to rest on your belly and your left hand to rest on your heart. It can also feel delicious to place a blanket over the belly or pelvis.

Breathe. Allow. Be here for 5-10 minutes (or for as long as you possibly can).

STAR POSE

The beauty of this shape is that you can practice it anywhere.

Begin in a standing position, with your feet about hip distance apart. Notice the feeling of the ground underneath your feel, of your spine, and of the lift of the crown of your head.

Gently widen your stance, with your feet just slightly wider than hip distance. As you feel the support and rootedness of your legs, reach your arms up and out.

As you breathe in, feel rooted in your feet and legs. As you exhale, allow your aliveness to travel up and out from your heart through your hands and fingertips.

Stay here for a few rounds of breath or until your heart smiles.

ACKNOWLEDGEMENTS

I am so grateful. So very grateful.

As I sit here and realize that with these acknowledgements, my book will be finished...my delight meter is off the charts. So I should probably begin my thanks to the patrons of the coffee shop that couldn't help but smile as I raised my arms and did a little dance in my seat.

This book would not have been a thing without the many people in my life, from clients to mentors, to friends, who made me realize and celebrate the fact that I've always been a nudger.

Bringing this book forward now, in 2021, fills me with ALL the THINGS. It comes after several years of overthinking. Who, me? Write a book? And a lot of "I don't know what I would write about...". And then something happened. I actively and intentionally started cultivating my creativity, reconnecting with my body as my source of wisdom, and exploring the full range and value of my voice.

And voila...here we are.

But this wouldn't be possible without a few folks in particular.

My incredible and courageous clients for allowing me to be a nudger and for doing the transformational work to inhibit their thriving.

To Michelle Barry Franco, Barbara McAfee, and Susan Hyatt for helping me inhabit my voice, my delight, and the power of my inner fire.

To Heather Winia for introducing me to a newfound sense of freedom in my body that makes my heart smile.

To the RLP summer camp crew for all the things.

To Holly, my favorite and best Om-ie and giggle sister. I love you.

To Jessica for being my Tiny Book sister and friend.

To Julia Cameron's *The Artist's Way*, Patti Digh's *Creativity Is a Verb*, and Kaira Boston for being my creativity mentors.

(And, ahem, to Kaira Boston for her artistry and willingness to allow my crazy ideas to become fabulous realities. How much do we LOVE the yin yoga shape drawings???)

To my Peloton bike for being my best investment EVER and the incredible instructors like Robin Arzon, Christine D'Ercole, and Matt Wilpers that inspire and push me every single time I get on the bike.

To the Mandarin Oriental DC (and the Washington DC Tidal Basin) for being the inspiration I didn't even realize I needed.

To the Arenal Volcano and rainforest in Costa Rica for the masterclass in aliveness as a warmup to writing this book.

To my parents. For all the things. My dad for always seeing through my words and hearing the truth in my voice. My mom for your resiliency, stubbornness, and strength. And your chocolate mousse.

My brother for being my cheerleader, always.

For family near and far for reminding me of who I am, where I belong, and helping me find my way home when I feel lost.

To Nonna Elena, Nonna Sandra, and Nonna Dina for being strong and courageous — and teaching me to believe in possibility.

To Jupiter for reminding me that delight is everywhere.

To Simon for allowing me to birth one crazy idea after another and loving me in the way that only you can.

And to Samantha. Oh my Principessa. My Simah Chava — life's treasure. You became my teacher when the doctors first noticed you growing inside me. Thank you.

ABOUT THE AUTHOR

Elena Sonnino is a life coach, yin yoga teacher, and speaker. But what most people say about Elena is that she brings delightful sparks of energy to everything she does.

Elena is on a mission to help you transform the walls of survival mode into doors of possibility so that you can thrive as your most grounded and nourished self. Her work helps you get out of your head and into your body as your source of wisdom, and moves you from beyond shoulds and into delight, one day at a time.

At home, Elena enjoys watching the sunrise, tending to her many, many plants, riding her Peloton bike, impromptu kitchen dance parties, and sweating out all the things in her infrared sauna.

Her work has been featured by the Rancho La Puerta Wellness Resort and Spa, the Four Seasons Hotel Washington DC, Tiny Buddha, and the Chopra Center.

Learn more about Elena at www.elenasonnino.com.

www.ingramcontent.com/pod-product-compliance
Lightning Source LLC
Chambersburg PA
CBHW011239120626
46549CB00009B/3339